Words of the Day

Doggerel

Brian Jobe

Korrektiv Press

Seattle   New Orleans   Copenhagen

The cover was designed by Nathan Vass. The illustration is a detail from *L'embarquement pour Cythère*, by Jean-Antoine Watteau for his admission to the Royal Academy of Painting and Sculpture in 1717. Author photo by Nathan Vass.

Words of the Day

Preface

After subscribing to the Word of the Day email from *Dictionary.com*, I tried to write a sentence to remember the meaning of each daily word. That evolved into the practice of writing a short poem every day. I followed only one rule: an end rhyme had to be found for each Word of the Day. I think the first one I ever wrote was the one about General Custer at Little Big Horn (page 57). It isn't earth shaking, but there was something so pleasing in the rhyme that I kept at it. As the days passed, some got a little better, and family and friends seemed to enjoy reading them. Soon I had enough for a book, and then a bigger book. Readers might try writing a few of their own — it's a habit formed easily enough, and there are certainly worse ways to spend one's days.

Being words of the day, some of the vocabulary was a tad difficult (for me, anyway), so I decided to add a Glossary at the back of the book. The definitions are taken from *Dictionary.com*, but in order to save space I condensed them when I could.

Brian Jobe

in memoriam

FR JY OSB

The esse
of our esse
is to bless
this esse.

At a Motel Near the Airport
As one fly said to the other on a strip of glue,
"Nice place you picked for our rendezvous."

Moral Sentiments, Imaginary Beings
Adam Smith learned from François Quesnay
that if *laissez faire et laissez passer,*
le monde va de lui meme! An Invisible Hand to favor
industry and more productive labor,
with an Impartial Spectator to fairly examine
our pursuit of ever more mammon.
i.m. Howard E. Schmidt

On Day N° 9,127 in the Desert ...
With his magic staff/viper, sly Moses
struck a rock and drew forth water.
The Israelites slaked their thirst,
but as the days grew hotter
their good mood was dispersed
by kvetching about the hyperhidrosis.
for David Broudy

His Favorite Foreign Movies
Nathan watched all his favorites from Cannes, flick after flick after flick, until his eyes were xanthic.

On the Oregon Trail
When the Native Americans set fire
to the settlers' covered wagon,
Zachariah tried to play flapdragon
with his own funeral pyre.

Ascension and Fall
Theophilus Jr. was quite happy
to let go of his balloon,
but as he watched it evanesce
into the grey afternoon
he knew he'd have an even less
lovely day. Even crappy.

Fourth and Many, Again

I know this sounds lame,
maybe even a little impolitic,
but the name of the game
is *not* to give the ball a kick.
i.m. Mark Carolus

It's a Question of Principle
Marketing's ability to aggrandize
the worth of both buyer
and seller determines the brand size.
How do we determine desire?

She Herself Enjoyed a Glass of Wine
But every date they'd had so far was a vinous
affair of inebriated intimacy — a big minus.

Rum and Non-Dairy
After a little practice
he made a Moosemilk
potable for the lactose
intolerant: Use Silk.

On Trying to Read Heidegger's *Being and Time*
What is worth noting about such rarefied
reasoning is that so much needs to be clarified.
for Richard Polt

On Trying to Read *Der Spiegel*
German words can be mega long,
the simplest speech sprechgesang.

Trouble

Sometimes it comes on like a tidal
wave; sometimes it seems to sidle.

Kim Il-Sun, Jong-il, and Jong-un
How long can the Pyongyang trinity
be extended through consanguinity?

As the Planet Spins
From one word to another during these doggerel
days of summer, like painted horses on a carousel.

The First Rule of Contemporary Living
At all times you should rush hither
and yon, and never, ever dither.

Portrait of Mom at Fifty-seven
In the end, she was happy to jilt
the man who wore a utility kilt.

On the Blue Ocean Floor
SpongeBob likes to play matador
with a bikini top and an albacore.

At the Bakery Counter
When the Old Fart griped and tried to finagle
more change, Finkelstein just held up a bagel.

Do Not Emit Too Much Carbon

"We're a mess", went
the old refrain. And for the sanctity
of the viridescent
there's a new version of chastity.

A Very Short History of Europe and the Levant

The Crusades are almost universally despised
as a battle between the drunken larrikin
raping and pillaging under the flag of The Baptized
and the innocent and honorable Saracen.

Success & Safety
Those who would like to accrete
will find it helps to be discreet.

Kingdoms of Darkness
Thomas Hobbes' *Leviathan*, named
for an unspecified thalassic
monster, is a political science classic,
but can it perhaps be blamed,
even partly, for the miserable fates
of so many modern states?

Babies Take Notice
Vomiting all over your layette
is actually good etiquette.

A Totem vs Herbert the Slug

I thought I'd be able to stymie
Snyder, but he blew right by me.

Impenetrability!
To maintain his lofty self-regard, the poetaster
keeps repeating, "Such a one is to be master."

A Wife with a Knife
By far the most woeful and despised gobbet
was the far-flung penis of John Wayne Bobbit.

Don't Do It
Whosoever seeks a vocation to scribble
will soon learn to quibble. And fribble.

Blight of the Fumblebee

For "Flight of the Bumblebee",
his own rifacimento,
with a just little less honey,
and a lot more lento.
for Miyo Aoki

Rolling Stoned
Did all those drugs for the Glimmer Twin
make life more or less Sisyphean?

I Am Not What I Am
Did not Siddhartha, under the boh tree,
hear something like Iago's ploce?

Gastric Japanese Plastic
Half an egg, a chicken thigh,
and a tower of noodles soaring high
up to a pair of chopsticks
floating in the air, the entire mix
graced with a green garnish —
all of it fake, and covered in varnish.

Song to Walt Whitman
Won't this barbaric yawp
ever stop?

Be the Man Who's Havering

She'll be kicking it in the country,
and say, "Come, sweet Beau!"
Desire cannot stand the dilatory,
so if your wheels won't go,
your feet need to finish the story.
after Ovid, Ars Amatoria, *229-230*
for Stephen Hinds

Howard Loved the Desert

He didn't need nice. A Gobi, a
Mojave, a Bonneville Salt Flat —
anywhere his mysophobia
might be mollified, he was at.

Internal Eternal Recursion
Inside even the sorriest blighter
is an even sorrier writer.

Discipline and Begging for Attention

Needing others to need him, the dandy
feigns indifference, his modus operandi.
for Trevor Merrill

Diana's Rum Coffee

A better drink in winter you will not find:
along with fresh coffee, she gives you rum,
sugar, cinnamon, cloves, an orange rind,
and more sugar … ends in a tasty residuum.
for Teresa Lawrenson

My Onychomycosis

It takes a lot of chutzpa
to walk into a foot spa.

for Frederick Leaf

Can't Stand Ads for Antidepressants

Vilify
Abilify.
for Rex Gentry

Drinking to the Apocalypse
I prefer my pickle
to be rather brickle,
not to mention mickle,
with glass of George Dickel.
About this, I am not fickle,
and refuse to stickle.
Sometimes green juice will trickle
from my lips, then tickle
my chin, like a shiny new sickle
made out of nickel.

Beer is So Much Better on Tap
Stretched out across the bar, mouth on spigot,
he drank enough to float a frigate.

A Clean, Unlighted Place
To complain about the subfuscous
lighting doesn't do the pub justice.
for Bob Garrecht

Big Time Wrestling

While watching one character pretend to lam
into another, we pretend it isn't a sham.
i.m. Dusty Rhodes

Also in the Midst of the Garden
It teems with every arboreal
beast (e.g., chameleon, squirrel, sloth)
that feast with far more zeal
on fruit than Adam, sans tablecloth.

Dieting & Wretchedness
Her bigger ration
accompanied a familiar song,
the verbigeration
"It's wrong, wrong, wrong!"

The Battle of Little Big Horn
With every warrior he could muster,
Sitting Bull slaughtered General Custer.

Hunger Game
A dozen pigeons, fighting for a crumb
on the sidewalk, form a scrum.

High Hatted Smart Guy
If you have to commit *lèse-majesté*,
you ought to plan for amnesty.

Nude Model
The tattooed dude wearing a snood
appears to be a prude *and* lewd.
for Terentius Brown

The Best of the Amazing Lyre Bird
It's not just mating songs and caws
he must learn: quack, moo, purr … cries
of monkeys, cameras, chainsaws —
all these the little bird can vernacularize.
for Nathan Vass

Her Majesty's Exile Ends
His strategy was keen:
he sacrificed one pawn, won
back a lost queen,
and then exacted his wanion.

Report from Nepal
Hilly landscape — Everest is a dilly
of a climb. Rather chilly.
for Herb Rice

No Ifs, Ands, Ors, Buts About It
Something was missing. Nora pinned it on
the Greek, definitively: Asyndeton!
for Traci Sims

If He Has Plenty of Cash in Hand
Will the old stripper wrap her
self around the young whippersnapper?

Life After Life After Life
How can there be a fair God? We sense
something wrong in our clairaudience.

On October 20, 1967
Near Bluff Creek, California,
the sásq'ets was yclept
Bigfoot, as attested by a plaster cast
where he stepped.
after Roger Patterson & Robert Gimlin

Memoirs of the Jacobites
As soon as the bailiff got out, "Prithee,
friend", said he,
"what is it that hangs upon yonder tree?"
after Katherine Thomson

Don't Mind the Daily Grind
Some folks are just happy on the job, jolly
as a hog in a loblolly.
for Sheila Williams

The Empress Needs New Clothes
"An eight!" proclaimed Her Eminence
(although she had last been an eight-
een), forgetting how greatly the immense
glory of her personage doth emanate.

Modern American Politics

That every argument is, to the other side,
smoke and mirrors concealing pure greed
ought to unite us in alarm at the instauration
of a new era: straw men in a straw nation.

Behind the Jets
Across the wild blue yonder,
all those long contrails
in the sunset — try to ponder
them as pink, fluffy tails.
for Jack Halpin

Rock Stars & Professional Athletes
Led from A to B by their glans,
these fellows seem to have a Jovian
disposition toward their fans.
The truth is probably more Pavlovian.
after Bill Bradley

In Dancing Class
Art was a bit of a clod,
Tina tended to gangle,
so whenever they danced
they called it "Tangle".

Jesus, Emerson, Nietzsche, Buddha
With verbiage like pelage in a pillow, the pastor
filled his philippic—a true philosophaster.

The Secretary to the Bishop of Hippo
was greatly blessed.
Setting down the stylus, and rubbing his wrist,
the famulus
winced and muttered, "Damn you, Gus!"
for J.K. Tanner

According to the Witch Doctor
For most infections, use moss. An obeah
for mental problems, such as nosophobia.

One or Two Latin Terms
He complained when she wouldn't accept
what he offered as pabulum;
she offered then that he was hardly adept,
her own *argumentum ad baculum*.

Land of the Free: The Story of Stalking Cat
After talking it over with his Tribal Chief,
Dennis decided to follow the Way of the Tiger.
A psychiatrist might diagnose zoanthropy,
but this new kitten decided he was no man. So he
had surgeons do some work *à la* feline motif:
implanted whiskers, a bifurcated lip, pointed ears,
a lot of tattooed stripes (he didn't buy fur),
and the final touch: teeth filed sharp as shears.
i.m. Dennis Avner

A Bass Explains His Aversion to Eating Worms
With a hook still in his mouth, "Just as I felt one long tug, I thought, I need a new Weltanschauung!"

Poor Yorick, Doomed to a Melancholic Rant
If he'd blathered on over any number
of other skulls, he might have lost his nostomania:
the sullen, the prideful, the loyal — all slumber
as well, but the Prince must have tossed the crania.

Solander in the British Museum

"Nature loves to hide," Heraclitus
wrote, thinking of plants or rocks
or perhaps of this or that creature.
But humans also belong to nature,
and so we let our Nature guide us,
even in the library, devising a box
to store the miscellaneous supplies
and papers of a naturalist. Candor
isn't as vital as practical in the guise
of a book, thence called a solander.

for Jonathan Potter

News, Commercials, and ... Repeat
You would think that news anchors
and advertisers are paid just to gaslight
their audiences, unloading rancors
and products for mass mental blight.

Hungry Birds
With his powerful, hooked beak, the griffin
draws sparks as he quarries gold for a tiffin.

At $250, You Can't Beat the Sassicaia
As the freshly vinted oenophile began to degust
the cabernet, the sommelier prayed, "Be just!"
for Nicolaas Wilkins & Cameron Campbell

A Different Emma Crosses Oklahoma
Driving 2,500 head of cattle over Chisholm
Trail required a certain measure of bovarism.

Vicious and Superstitious

An auger watching the flight paths of birds
might as well look at turds,
a haruspex can't really see the future quiver
in bird guts or a sheep liver,
and determining guilt seems awfully chancy
in resorting to alphitomancy.
i.m. Brian Donaher

Supernatural Selection in Oregon
The young poet, effectively banished
from his kingdom, continued writing
and chasing butterflies — twice Joy
compensated him for the vanished
land of his language. Every sighting
of a lepidopteran brought him home
to a renewed reality, the aging viceroy
ever inscribing the luminous gloam.
i.m. Vladimir Nabokov

Geometry Final
The student unable to draw a quincunx
flunks.
for Keith Himmelman

The Three Word Version
A coach and an umpire
began an urgent colloquy:
the one first musing
about the other's own desire,
that other refusing
one's untendered apology.
after Charles Krauthammer

Even the Devil Seems on the Level
To avoid war, Daniel Webster tried
compromising with the southern states
by passing the Fugitive Slave Law.
He lived just two more years, but saw
his politics fail — saw how even greats
can't see through the dark of vespertide.
i.m. Shelby Foote

The Meat Locker
The new True TS-23F-HC Freezer
is truly frigorific—
you'll need a saw for this here
chilly pig, or a pick.

A Dozen Drinks Later at the Club
He noticed beneath his fez a very numb
buzzing had drowned out his desiderium.

Stone Tablets, Codices, or eBooks
Whichever you prefer, but we'll all agree
that what we want is more philology.
i.m. Robert Renehen

Young Bacchus, Bitten by a Lizard
It wasn't just bad PR plus zero
support from Cesari — Amerighi lacked
self-control and a sense of tact
from the start. But, oh, the chiaroscuro!
for Robert Hardgrave

A Long Engagement & Estrangement
He flatters himself, and she plays
along with it—maybe they were star-crossed
from the start. So love decays
like a tree with termites, and years are lost.

Adrift on a Sea of Shame
As if they could siphon
an ocean empty, the pubescent
lads work overtime,
their hairless cheeks rufescent.

"Does Anyone Care for Bread?"
Vegans every one, the highfalutin'
at table nine were still panivorous,
so the entire group asked in chorus,
"Yes, but does it have any gluten?"

Decapitalization as Ontology
Reichenbach invented a force
of nature and named it the od:
a power that runs the universe,
as basic as taking G from God.
after Baron Carl von Reichenbach

A God of Morality May Seem Like a God of Cruelty
In the order of nature, arousal
Comes long before espousal.

For Expensive Pearls
There's no better cloister
than the original oyster.

A Winter's View of Autumn
Following September,
orange October guided
a more boreal November,
bister, brisk, and sobersided.

Presence & Abscess
Instead of white there,
there was just a square,
black space—odontoid.
Empty. So gone. Void.
for Bryn Halpin

007 Escapes Again
As Bond jumped from the plane, some were stunned
to see a parachute fly out of his cummerbund.
after Ian Fleming

A Tree, a Swan and a Mirror
Gliding under a willow,
an otherwise immobile cygnet
watched his twin follow
beneath, do a quick jig ... sit.

Hiking in the Blue Mountains
Sitting on a log, I heard
a footfall behind me stop. I rose
slowly, turned and saw
the sásq'ets, malodorous and pilose.

The Suburban Caves of Mystery
A burnt-out bulb
in a basement packed with junk,
means that to find the furnace,
you need to spelunk.

Man's Best Friend's Personal Assistant
Holding a warm bag,
he watched his collie wag
her tail
at the end of the trail,
then lollygag.
for Chester Halpin

If the Ocean is Empty
Certain lads need,
for a certain kind of lassie, an
approach or a deed
that is more Parnassian.

Rhyme Fiction
This is a true story —
it's a real humdinger —
a man was for himself
his own dumb ringer.
after Jim Thompson

Biologically Speaking
It must suck to be a monad,
since you have no gonad.

Fear the Plague
Never let
a leveret
into Everett.
for Peter Jackson

David Hume Recalls Charles Boyle
I speired him thareanent heiven, for a wee
bairn I was, dumfoondered at his orrery.

Fight Fire with Fire
Whenever he went to church,
he lit an entire row of votive
candles — avoiding the lurch
into Hell was his only motive.
for Marianne Jackson

The Passing of the Passenger Pigeon

Ectopistes Migratorius is now extinct.
Gone. Flock
after flock once darkened the sky,
then died en bloc.
for Ted & Barbara Rothstein

So Not Happening at the Zoo
You'll have to forgive the elephant,
if his manner seems a bit brusque:
imagine a runny nose in that trunk,
let alone a toothache in his tusk!
after Paul Simon

Which Shall Fulfil All My Will

He simultaneously had complete faith in dogma (key to orthodoxy) and his own frailty (i.e., cacography).

Machiavelli's Power

Only a devil could,
gleeful, scrawl so bleak
a *speculum principium*
of pure realpolitik.

Proper Denunciation

Pronouncing French
makes my mouth clench,
and words in German
are difficult to determine,
while so rapid is Spanish
that it seems to vanish.
Words sound like mush in
my mouth, if Russian,
and it's best there aren't so
many to hear my Esperanto.
Just for fun, query an
expert about my Hungarian.
My mistakes in Italian
could form a battalion
and just hearing Chinese
makes my brain freeze —
all this is why I am a fan
of ASL (or "Ameslan").
for Eligius Carter Halpin

Takeru Kobayashi Maru
Yes, I want another hot dog,
and I also want this chili. Want
this beer, too. Then I'll beg
to lie on the floor, dissilient.
i.m. Masaki Kobayashi

Fashion Their Passion
"Well! You certainly have a fine
looking tie, M. Blass," said M. Saint
Laurent, fluffing his own pavonine
ascot, he himself looking *très bien*.
for Kent Worthington

At the Market
Look at your betting
on stocks and shares
as the perfect bletting
of Bartlett pears.
for Rick Shelby

A Toddler Has Got to Know His Limitations
After a few hours on the seesaw, Timothy
had a hard time maintaining his equanimity.

An Imaginary Hen
If you cannot jog
on one leg
you can still joggle,
just as you can boo
God
in the glen
of a boondoggle,
but if you go
and growl
at the hens,
do not imagine
it is only the hen
you can hornswoggle.

New Layer for the Mayor
When J.P. joined the sewing klatsch,
he learned to sew on his own patch.
i.m. Chris Wedes

The Beginning of a Long Riddle
Because Richard grew up in the middle,
he was always good at telling the taradiddle.

Don't Stir Up the Dust!
On the savannah, a spindly-legged,
galloping camelopard
dwarfed a nearby zebra, who begged
her not to trammel so hard.

The Frustration of a Bad Installation I
Exactly where wall
to wall carpeting will eventually rimple
isn't so simple,
creating conditions for a dangerous fall.

24 Carat, Hand Woven, $19,000
From Mr Kennedy,
the most ridiculous swag yet:
a pair of gold shoelaces,
each with a gold aglet.

The Greenest Acre

Her saving grace
has been a lambent
sense of humor,
always useful for
when unable to place
where her ram went.

The Frustration of a Bad Installation II
That rimple in the rug where
he always tripped was a real bugbear.

Again the End of Him
She knew it had to be a con
when he said, "I'll call anon!"

A Very Fallow Field

Where best to bury an agrarian?

Woodworking 101
He took a lot of flak
for that spice rack.
for Ted Dorland

Always More to the Story
Re: their daughter and the groom,
Dad had a shrewd sense
of when who had screwed whom.
Mom tried to show prudence.

Hot Day, Cold Beer

He tried to stop,
but guessed the weight
would only drop
if he could estivate.

On Whether or Not to Go to the Nude Beach
I'd rather my cock got caught in a faulty zipper
than have it bit by a gallinipper.

The Cares of an Egyptologist
"Yes and No", he said with a cough. "Ka outlives life — an immortal scofflaw."

A Bored Lover Seeks Novelty

The mares seemed so last year,
so the stud mused, "That zedonk
on the far side of the pasture
has one hell of a bedonkadonk."

Deconstruct This
How high he climbed up a tree
in his study, *Of Grammatology*!
after Jacques Derrida

In Praise of *Brevitas* & *Concinnitas*
Every reader's plight:
at times even the best writers gloze
over their own insight
with descriptions in stultifying prose.

Recover Everything You Can
The stroke had bizarre
effects: made it difficult to walk,
and impossible to talk
coherently. But damn! You went
for broke on foot—far
and wide, once more ambulant.

Honky Tonk Men
Singing like Buck Owens sang,
Dwight Yoakam
added an accordian to the twang
for a touch of hokum.

Damn that Wily Odysseus!
said Poseidon in a strident
tone, brandishing his trident.
"Just, damn ..." said Calypso
watching the raft he grips go.

Cooperative Hunting

Some roving Coralgroupers nod
at a school of Giant Moray
Eels, inviting the double-jawed
serpents to a feeding foray
in the reef — to flush out every niche,
to kill their prey with a twitch.

Halftime
He approached the larder
with great ardor.

End of the Pushmi-pullyu
Dolittle had a kind of twin llama, double-
headed, but without an ass.
Yet the need to poop is indomitable —
so where went the grass?

Sophia Appears in Human Form

Wisdom needs us to be wise.
Not just wants, but actually needs,
first revealed in human deeds,
then in words. But we barricade Her
behind our desires, and our lies
cover her truth: *Homo prevaricator*.
after Harry Frankfurt

Selves Inflated by Idle Talk

Gerede comes in many
colorful flavors: some prate
on and on, others repeat
what others repeat, cut–rate —
None of it worth a penny,
but every one free to retweet.

after Martin Heidegger

Crabby Limit

He's allowed to trap two. Less
if he's crapulous.

for Eric Voldal

Santa Barbara Twilight
Phosphorus in the foaming
waves at the edge of the sea
glowed in the dark gloaming,
and illuminated your knee.

Banking on the Bureaucracy
Once based on industry, my annuity
was endangered by the tenuity
of recent returns. A new perpetuity
based on taxes suits me to a T.

Make Way for the Dandelions
She always tried to acquiesce
to whatever would effloresce.

How Many People, Ever?
From Adam to today's
seven billion, in toto? Vast
the number descended
from that protoplast.
after Charles Darwin

Wahlberg's Good Vibrations
We all have to start somewhere,
so bringing up "Marky
Mark" and the underwear ads
isn't necessarily snarky.

Shifting Borders Among German Speaking Peoples from Archaic Times to the Present

Hops the men grew for beer the men pissed
were reason enough for any irredentist.

Staring into the Void
Brainwave-wise, it's much the same: gnaw pen
caps or meditate on your mat, sitting zazen.
after D.T. Suzuki

In Whose Interest?
The shelves of Walmart and Target
will be forever laden
with more and more stuff made in
China, for our debt.

No Secrets Allowed
Security furtively mic'd
up all the powder
rooms, because they liked
to spy on the clowder.

Time for a Trip to the Dump
As she saw the garage
turn into an omnium-gatherum
of uselessness, we saw
mom become rather glum.

How to Become a Prodigal Son
Dream of a distant country,
make a wish, mock a
father's prayer,
and break with your mishpachah.

Unsentimental Education
A timid lad often shuns,
when he really ought not avoid, in
certain social situations,
the more aggressive hoyden.
after Henry Fielding

The Spider at the Gates of Dawn
In autumn there is little awesomer
than the sight of light on so much gossamer.

The Hapless Heist on All Hallow's Eve

The two had a plan, even a sense of irony.
They wore masks of Shaggy and Freddie
in case of cameras. Cut the bolt. Their heist
was some silverware and costume jewelry
thrown into a pillow case—fairly petty—
and … beer from the fridge. Tomfoolery
to fall asleep, drunk in front of the TV,
to be unmasked like any cartoon poltergeist.
after Joe Ruby & Ken Spears

The Barbecue Pit's Sweet, Sweet Style

With awe, she regarded my bib—awe, pity
and even distress at my swelling gibbosity.

for Pitmaster Pookie

You Are What You Eat
Said I to self, licking my thumb,
"It's hard to disambiguate
between the pig you've become
and this damn pig you ate."

Keep the Appearance of Beings in Mind

It might be a surprise to hear hunger simulate
thunder, or to see a flash of forked lightning
that resembles tree roots or the laciniate
edges of a leaf, but the most frightening
thing about nature isn't a simple brute fact,
but how it forms with thought a perfect pact.

for Brittany Hammer

Like Quills Upon the Fretful Porpentine
Spirits, ghosts, souls of the dead — their glorification
by the living leads to plenty of horripilation.

Summarizing the Field Notes

Have them do whatever they'd better do, then mix that with wherever they'd best do it. Euthenics.

When in Glasnevin
On St. Patrick's Day
you should wear a green
shirt, pants, or a tie —
you won't look so peregrine.

Warming and Herbs

They say that beforetime
You could see more rime
on rosemary or thyme.
for Bjørn Lomborg

Rhyme for *The Unreality of Time*
Past, Present and Future,
according to Professor McTaggart,
are merely a mental suture
holding together with the tenses
the experience of our senses,
in a manner opposite a braggart.

Rite as Rain
The priest used an evergreen branch to sparge
them with showers, which were rather large.
for Fr Michael Ryan

The Man Who Swallowed an Ocean
The flesh eaten right off Santiago's skeleton
became the villager's favorite feuilleton,
but who knows what monsters from the deep
swam up to appear in Papa's sleep.
after Ernest Hemingway

The Dragon at Peace
From any point of view on the xyst,
one rock or another will be missed.
after Akisato Ritō

Marking the Spot
Names were often difficult to chase
down, but on a last recon
he even found for *X Fretensis* a place
in his original *Onomasticon*.
after Eusebius

Circus of Envy
Regarding others regard the bel-esprit,
he was always overcome by jealousy.

Mnemosyne Looks Backwards

I've never met a
muse that wasn't somehow meta.

Friedrich Nietzsche
was quite the gnomist,
but life wasn't peachy
with thought missed.

Life Curled Under a Heat Lamp
Stirring from sleep, his penultimate
action was to eat living mice. Creepy.
He may decide to then molt. A pet
snake is mostly boring. And sleepy.

Listening to Grandma
The woman was loquatious
to a degree truly bodacious.
i.m. Elsie Jobe

As a Flower of the Field, So He Flourisheth
We know how the death of Absalom riled King
David, the son plucked from life like a wildling.

Commas Must Be Inside Quotation Marks
The editor is a fan of punctuation,
but this commitment is a sad comma, on him.
I think I prefer ad hominem
attacks to nitpicking nincompoopery. It's more fun.

Had He Killed Moby Dick
Ahab would have had to buy a pan
to fry up all that leviathan.
for Matthew Lickona

Advising Virtue
Grandpa said, "Marry an abecedarian."

Hurt by *Urtica Dioica*
After stinging nettle soup and stinging nettle
salad, my stung stomach just wouldn't settle.

The San Patricio Rattlesnake Races
The snake able to most quickly slither, wins---
as long as it doesn't start withershins.

Wild Mountain Rhyme
Never tire of the day
as it breaks over an adret,
and may it then bring you back
to the cool of the ubac.
for Timothy Paul Jobe

Trouble in Tahiti
Art and Tina's increasingly apparent schism
began with the onset of his tarantism.

Another of its Discontents
It's a convenient quirk
of civilization that to be vain
doesn't mean you're not sane.
Just try not to be a jerk.

Downwind in Steeleville, MO

Because of a strong zephyr,
we could easily smell the heifer.
i.m. Paul & Lois Gamble

Hemingway's Law
The clearer the diction,
the richer the fiction.

That Fat Cat Doesn't Need You
Don't bother talkin'
To that old grimalkin!
i.m. Smoke

As in Women's Clothing
What succeeds, what fails?
The line between frippery
and well-wrought details
can be somewhat slippery.

The Princess Looks in the Mirror
At the moment of anagnorisis
she was neither a hag, nor a miss.

More Trouble in Tahiti
The only interference
with Art's dearly held meliorism
was the steady reappearance
of that damned tarantism.

Nagoya, Japan, 1987

After college I was hard struck
with a severe bout of wanderlust.
I went East (directionally, west)
and there, with a kind of luck,
found that the past is yonder, rust
eternal, but the present blessed.
for Tatsie Shibata

A Contemptuous Crowd
Sally, Dick, Jane and even Spot
are somewhat more blamed
for simply being what we are not.
No harm to the forenamed.

Bellevue, Washington, 1988
At dusk, I'd sit on the back porch watching bats flit through the trees. Which they never, ever hit.

Convalescent Def Clique
Her latest coterie
Was made up of boys
From the Rotary
Club. Hence the noise.

Mounting a Master

If you want a passé-partout
for a picture frame,
it's okay to use a faster glue,
but to steal the same …
for a key, some plaster, too.

The Stoic Imagination
Imagine, for the Cosmos,
that we live in a gargantuan,
black plastic garbage bag.
The gods therefore ventilate
our world through pinholes,
and thus the stars scintillate.

A Romantic Scene

Cue crescent
moon. Spumescent
waves, incessant.
A soft breeze, then quiescent.
Effervescent.

Fun is Also Real
Even the Solemn should frivol
once in a while. It's only civil.

Planned Bachelorhood

Said the lonely bachelor: "If I had
a wife, I would be half of a dyad.
If we had a child, we'd be a triad.
Another… I think I like my pad!"
for Troy Collotzi

The Great One
As slippery as oil on ice,
Gretzky could deke
opponents twice, thrice —
gone in a blue streak!

Vodka & Gatorade
Not exactly immiscible,
but a little too pissable.

Batter Up
After *almost* all the goop
was gone, it was hardly picayune
for me to lick the spoon
and beaters as I cleaned the stoup.

Reflection on Necessary Being
Hinting at something ethereal
(otherwise they would refer
to the being of a brain), *noetic*
leaves out something, material
maybe, for which some prefer
the more muscular word *poetic*.

Jackson's Gnomic Actions

By circling and swaying,
swinging, flinging, and spraying,
dripping and throwing
down colors onto a field so thick,
pure light began flowing
back into his brain, achromic.
i.m. Jackson Pollock

A Very Muddy Trail
Emma and Co. had to cuittle
the cattle into fording
the river. Every dung beetle
was given free boarding.

April Greets Lord Elmsworth with a Practical Joke
They were able to move his beloved Bentley
to a spot next to the dumpster with a sneaky tow
truck, complete with a banana peel, gently
placed on the hood—some fool's idea of a capriccio.
after P.G. Wodehouse

Even the Fairways Are Just Brutal
For trouble with the wood
he had a little pill. That this could do his
confidence so much good
made it necessary—even prelusive.

Judgement Call
The most successful fib
is somewhat glib.

Lewis & Clark, November 3, 1805
Not very many have canoed
through such a vastitude.

Heard Between the Cracks in a Sidewalk

So said what had only just been a seed: "Can't let
a little cement get in the way of this plantlet!"
for Maggie Willson

Finishing the Fibonacci Sequence

To the right of one and one, add in the right sum.
Then add those two last numbers, ad infinitum.
for David Hedlund

The Family Heirlooms, a History
Seeing the furniture all chewed
up, Dad asked, "What sly dog have we
here?" One with a taste for wood,
who left his signature in xylography.

The Dance Contest Cuts
It was an old story:
Seeing the champions bedash
their dreams of glory,
Art and Tina did The Gnash.

Da Dum. Da dum. Da dum, Dadum Dadum ...
Beautiful colors won't stop Jaws. It ate
the girl without her bikini, pink and purple vittate.
after Roger Kastel

Meditating on His New Google Phone

Funny, how much some fellow's Nexus
phone posture resembles omphaloskepsis.

How to Succeed at Poetry

All you poets of this new age,
witty types who strut the stage,
introverts who won't get out,
extroverts who show no doubt—
let your guide be an ambivert
such as Namby Pamby—blurt
out your vices and lines no more,
polish them up, and don't bore!
after Henry Carey

Becoming Falstaff
After his weekly debauchery,
the young coxcomb
reconsiders life, his mockery
of it, and walks home.

Speculating About My Nieces' Future Hobbies
Some day, will Bryn
play Poker, or Gin
Rummy? Will Natalie
take up philately?

Nothing But a Vicious Rumor
Catherine was such a hippophile
she had to ice her lip a while.

"Saul, Saul, Why Do You Persecute Me?"
On the road to Damascus, the man from Tarsus
must have experienced a profound catharsis.

The Worst Thing I've Ever Witnessed
The engineers and craftsman were diligent,
certainly, but still the dirigible went
down in flames. We can only be so vigilant.
after Herb Morrison

The Impatient Cheapskate
"Where the hell is that damn bus? Fudge it!
I'll walk instead," said the fussbudget.

Can't Take Cary For Granted
Such a superb sense of style
is employed with a kind of guile.
after Roger O. Thorndike

S-A-M-M-A-M-I-S-H, Let's Go!

My high school, Sammamish,
had for its mascot the totem,
as in pole, but seeing as a mascot
is itself a kind of totem, or type,
one and many, both specimen
and species, I learned early not
to take competition and hype
too seriously, though now I wish
I had, a little more anyway, when
blood was young, yet pro tem.

In Vento et Rapida Aqua

Even if her words could be written
on wind and rapid water,
they were seductive and susurrant —
and electric. I sought her
again and again, wanting to be bitten
again, just to feel the current.

Jeeves
There was never a more fervent
(or at least a more faithful) servant.
after Stephen Fry

Józef Teodor Konrad Korzeniowski
After years at sea, he adapted a *nom*
de plume for English language readers,
still recognized as a Polish phenom,
among my favorite modern writers.
i.m. Val Foubert

A Sacred Moment of Love
Sometimes it must be now.
The moment when, er ... a bull
approaches his beloved cow —
it isn't always so venerable.

Magical, the Mischief
A little orange-bearded man
on the emerald isle of Eire
puffs on a white clay dudeen
stoking a little orange fire.

At This Size, You Have to Expect a Tight Fit
Muumuus only seem to run big. You fuss
over the colors, not that they're contiguous.

If You Want to Hike the A.T., aka the
Appalachian Trail, you should map a way from
3,782 ft Springer Mountain (in Georgia's
Chattahoochee forest) to the equally gorgeous
Mount Katahdin (a Penobscot appellation).
And the truly adventurous won't incur any fines
if they ditch the map and follow the signs.
for Reed and Jean Steele

Lepidus, Antony, and Octavian
Announcing the Lex Titia,
they commissioned themselves as a triumvirate
for restoring the Res Publica,
while in reality they did anything but.

Miss Marple Checks the Passenger Manifest
Once on board, she noted a wayfarer
or three who appeared suspicious: a fey wearer
of wing tips, a girl with a large trunk,
a professor-type in a pith helmet, and a monk.
after Agatha Christie

How Vulgar and Yet How Irresistible
It was as if the author had set up a trap. Clap
as they may, the audience knew it was claptrap.

What Seye We of Hem that Bileevin
Before the Retraction, anticipating the Scales,
the Parson tells us that nothing is more chancy
than Death, so forswear divynailes,
like trying to interpret dreams, or geomancy.

But No
Senior citizens, you would think,
should be hard to hoodwink.

Miki's Coach
Sato helped teach the gal how
to land a quadruple salchow.

The Greatest Metaphor
A bug may become a butterfly,
a frog, his plant.
All men one day die,
of which few are cognizant.

The Ultimate Fall Guy

For the CIA, in Dallas, Lee
Harvey Oswald
began what might be called
the conspiratorial fallacy.
after Don DeLillo

Beyond the Law of Laws
Even the most just law must
follow one still more august.
for Jean-Luc Marion

The Linguistics of Counterfactual History

If El Draque hadn't helped defeat the Armada,
if Napolean hadn't brokered *la Vente de la Louisiane*,
if *Das Dritte Reich* had led to a Deutsch lingua franca,
we might say, receiving *un vaso de agua*, "*Danke!*"
for Quinn Hallenbeck

Carlos Danger
Mock the poor dumb
cockalorum.

Touring the Co-ed Dorms

She was always sure to repeat,
"Some slob may not
lift the seat."
A most important caveat.

for Natalie Halpin

A Match Made for Burning
My ex is the epitome
of the type of gal to be rid of me.

Bubbles
"As if you need any help!" She liked to razz
him for always drinking wine *avec gaz*.

A Lark
That was a quite a conquest,
the poor author of that aubade
about waking in the dark,
believing he'd go to prison.
And did not. That's not so bad.
i.m. Robert Conquest & Philip Larkin

The Most Welcome Guest

He always praised the host.
He would never gripe, cuss, or list
off his achievements (most).
The man is a true deipnosophist.
for Braden Mechley

Another Invitation
Noticing that he'd grown
somewhat fusty
in recent years, she groaned
and said, "Must we?"

A Flood and a Baptism
Not so much a solemn sign
as joyful, even columbine.
for Reverend Horatio Yanez

To the Monsters Under My Bed
At the very least, ye scary
creatures belong in a bestiary.

Definitions & Metaphors

The place where a baby sleeps,
a translation for peeps,
or a verb meaning to steal. *Crib*.
A condom packed tight
with fake blood and dynamite,
or a display of wit. *Squib*.

A Match Made in Heaven
Jill loved Jack and Jack loved Jill.
Even if they were both uncouth, dumb
and a little crazy, each still
thought the other plenty toothsome.

23rd Century Technology Was So Slow

After flipping it open, Captain Kirk
waited for his communicator to chirk.

for William Shatner

Conversation in a Pet Store
A cat lover appears at the bell
over the doorway, in tears. Blinks.
"My — *atchoo!* — allergy hell,
triggered by fur." "Oh really? A
hairless feline can stop that sneeze.
Try the Canadian Sphynx,
perfect for people with allergies
and afflicted with ailurophilia."

Cadet and Commander
With her Shih Tzu on his arm, the ROTC cadet bowed and scraped for his schatzi.

In the Days of Noah
Because of our sins, the antediluvial
age gave way to one more pluvial.

It Pays to Believe, or At Least Play Along

There may or may not be a tooth
fairy, but cash is plenty sooth.

Anchorman
Dan Rather: quite
the blatherskite.

Ski to Die
It sure looked like trouble
as we watched him start to schuss
his way down the double
diamond slopes. Bill was no wuss!
i.m. Bill Johnson

At the Scrabble Convention
You'll find that some of the guys
would like to neologize.

Tools for the Fire
Downstairs we had a fireplace,
and in the inglenook
on the right stood a small shovel,
a broom, a brush, and a bellow.
On the left a tin vase,
and a poker with a single hook.

At the Very First 4th of July Picnic
The host announced to those about to eat,
"BBQ is served. Don't dally! Napkins
are in short supply. Latecomers will need
to use their petticoats and galligaskins!"

At the Two Hundredth 4th of July Picnic
The host couldn't drink enough to slake
his thirst after so much Shake 'n Bake.

Solomon Grundy, Scientist
The next-to-last calculation
made by this egg headed boffin
was to predict the durability
of a sealed polypropylene coffin.

Rhyming, Earlobes, and Destiny
When he saw his newborn baby,
the sad dad said, "I guess he'll
end up evil and depraved. Sessile
earlobes mean there's no maybe."

A Super Bowl of Bean Dip
The malodorous fug from
the couch was truly ugsome.

Never Write New Numbers on a Napkin
He sought her out in every boîte,
found nought, and became distraught.

The Banality of Banal
Even the finest meal ends up in the anal
Canal.

Real Men Are Meant to Work Outdoors
All the other jobs seemed to Hank pettifogging
chores compared to getting sweaty, logging.
after Ken Kesey

Churchill and Astor
With one riposte,
the other was toast.
For a moment at most.

Beginnings & Endings
For that first, lost syllable, the word *sample*
is an excellent example of aphesis,
not unlike apocope, when a Mrs (old, ample)
is remade (please don't laugh) a Miss.

Beauty Will Indict the World
There is a great and terrible beauty
preserved from the antebellum
South, in records kept for business
so elegantly written on vellum.
for Joshua Hren

Sue the Bastard
Her appetite for litigious
resolutions was prodigious.

The All Weather Walker
Her cheeks felt really, really raw
after walking a while in a williwaw.
for Jennifer Halpin

Same Old Same Old
Whether the reference is to ibid or idem,
if you want to know more, "Read 'em!"

In the Soup
Misology
leads to idolatry.

Keep Keeping It Real
In an age of camp and kitsch,
there is a slight hitch
in deciding what is truly echt:
best remain circumspect.

Theorem
Neither the infinite nor the infinitesimal
will you reach with yet another decimal.
after Soren Kierkegaard

Busking on a Sunday Afternoon
Fast and squirrelly notes
played by a man on a hurdy-gurdy
echoed throughout the park
over a droning much more sturdy,
if perhaps a tad less purdy.
for John Franklin

An Episode in Epic Mode
Homer's favorite bon mot —
murion legomenon — is "D'oh!"
after Matt Groening

Slicing Out of Bounds

After hacking his way free
of a man-eating bramble,
he got back on the fairway
with a wobbly wamble.
for Paul Steele

Doo After the Good and Leve the Evyl
Chivalry itself is more than fable,
even if modeled on knights in *Le Morte
d'Arthur*, and how they comport
themselves away from the round table.
for Richard & Idalla Jobe

Baumgartner's Fall
The balloon above shrank
to a pinpoint as he fell. Thin
air grew thicker, cushioning
his drop through the welkin.

Some Day
It is possible that a germ in us
will determine our terminus.
for Antonius Mulia

At a Competitive Eating Contest
A dozen hot dogs isn't just skosh
or a losing total, but *très gauche*.

From Hand to Mouth, If You Please
Intermission is snack time
for muppeteer and muppet,
bobbing for berries
right out of the punnet.
i.m. Jim Henson

Jealousy
How much he admired her well shod skill
at *les chassés et croisés* of the quadrille!

Historia Ecclesiastica Gentis Anglorum
In the 600s AD, the English
(Anglo-Saxons) had to cede
authority to Italian and Irish
missionaries — so says Bede.
for Abbot Jeremy Driscoll, OSB

Notes on Southey's *Madoc in Wales*
There is a very strange use of nomenclature:
Animated Beings are subject to Progression,
and Death, from which all things by Nature
are derived, exists in a Circle of Inchoation.

Reconsidering the Odds

Amidst a political dilemma
the AG decided to buckle,
but after avoiding that drama
and getting a bitter taste
of the future he soon faced,
he started to simply truckle.

Lois Loses with Long Odds
She began to drum her fingers and furrow
her brow — then laid down a Yarborough.
for Lois Gamble Duncan

Girder Meets Girdle
The poor guy nearly fell
when, after he cast an oeillade,
une femme tres belle
answered with a wink and a nod.

Winter Mornings in Transylvania
Mrs Dracula loved to hear
Mr (while he was enjoying his bowl
of fiber) Dracula hum
lullabies to their dear
vambini. Who then slept the whole
day in their hibernaculum.

In Stuffing or Greeting Cards
The worst of all the possible faults
is not using enough schmaltz.

The Most Wonderful Time of the Year
Korrektivians enjoy (being bad) Lent,
to Easter as to Christmas is Advent.
for everybody at Korrektiv

What Was the Question?
Frustration is a kind of riddle. Fix
it with ... Oh, fiddlesticks!

Training the Bartender
For a lime juice and rum
the fool used a jigger,
so I shoved it back at him
and asked for one bigger.

The Longest Day of the Year

She would not (this was one of her goals) miss
the sun rising or setting on the summer solstice.

for Faye Crow

Seattle Visitor's Bureau
There are too many bums,
damn few great
(i.e., one) museums,
but many places to ambulate.

Pleasure & Pain
So much carelessness took its toll: piss
burned. His penis required a poultice.

1066

Surprised by all those Normans, the Anglo-Saxon tribes might have fared better with a klaxon.

A Void
La Dispartition is a brilliant book, a long lipogram
that shuns a particular uncial. Nada. Zip. A lam.
après Georges Perec

Yosemite Sam Gets His Courage Up
Looking up at El Capitan,
playing it cool under an umbriferous
Black Oak … "Ooooh!
We won't let some cliff scare us!"
after Mel Blanc

Down on the Farm
On a page as white as milk, row
after row of black letters filled
a large field of text to be tilled
with red tools, such as a pilcrow.

Uncontainable Containers
Our lives we fill
with more and more largesse,
but who will finally pay the bill
is anybody's guess.

Flashy, Yes, But to What End?
Twirling a bottle of juice
with a flourish, he began to decant
the sour stuff into a shaker
with vodka, which seemed to be scant.

Memories of My Grandfather's Tools
An iron file with darkened grooves, sharp cusp
at one end, effective as a rasp despite the rust.

Beginning to See the Light
According to one theory
Life began with abiogenesis,
but even children know
there must have been a kiss.

Between North and South
East and West have met, and the twain
have found in each other much to gain.

Creature from the Black Lagoon Revisited
The scientist yelled, "This is no joke! Go! Run!"
as the Gill-man rose up out of the pokelogan.
after William Alland

McFadden's Blues
Searching for friends, the poor wight
gave them a fright!
after Seymour Reit & Joe Oriolo

Witnesses to the Catastrophe
"One second he was standing
there, at the edge of the kloof,
and the next it was, like, Poof!"
(quick nod at a likely landing).

Share the Road with Buses
The bicyclist moved over more for the big bus
and its engines rumbling like borborygmus.
for John Webb, Eddie Washington & Paul Margolis

Don't Give Me That Do Good Goody Good Bullshit
Before the credit and coinage of our current gelt
were bones and teeth and the occasional pelt.
after Roger Waters

First Prize at the *Twilight* 4-H Club
The kids from Gevaudan brought tethers
for a necklace made of mythical foofaraw:
ratatoskr skulls, a chupacabra tooth, the paw
of a jackalope, and lots of griffin feathers.

Any Way You Look at It, You Lose
They love their talking points, but are always wroth
to yield any time, their mouths marked with froth.

Almost Thanksgiving
First was Nicholas of Myra,
and then Kris Kringle, his antitype;
now we have Grinches hating Christmas
and all that Santa hype!

Cock-a-doodle-doo!
Pan stepped out of a dark forest
to greet the dawn, a foray
of blue into black, east to west,
and a red sun rose, con amore.

Crows to My Left, Crows to My Right

It's a wicked generation that looks for a sign, maugre
a plenitude of signs. And anyone can be an augur.
for Alyne de Winter

Scipio's Sidestep
The Carthaginians gathered at Zama were
defeated when Hannibal's elephants
failed to retreat, after charging the commissure
between columns of Roman grunts.
for Matthew Davis

326

To Cheat Defeat if Beat
It was more than bad luck
for the table when Ned, dick
that he was, pulled a frenetic
hand back from the muck.
for Chris Murray

Pocket Inventory
Rubber band, pen cap (no pen),
ticket stub, coin
(a nickel) ... and some lint,
which I here subjoin.

The Itch for Bait and Switch
Thy promises ring hollow,
but I fear Thy wrath. The bliss
that is supposed to follow
only increases my diathesis.

The Genocidal Heritage of Civilization
Before the siege of Béziers, the Catholic
faithful were asked to betray the Cathars.
They declined. Almaric, mirroring the gnostic
heresy neither tribe could abandon, gathers
his men, and commands: *Caedite eos
omnes. Novit enim Dominus qui sunt eius.*
for Ed Schramko

The Last in Line for Lunch During Lent
There were lots of greens left, but no fish. She ate
a salad, then, according to the rules of her novitiate.
for Anna Budinick

"Lieutenant Sulu, the con is yours!"
The helmsman found
the captain's chair, if not the captain
(when, say, Jim had to go
to the head) simpatico.
So when the captain, minus a pound,
returned, he zapped him.
for George Takai

Poem in Praise of My Sister
I know more than one lady
who esteems her own froideur;
they all seem a little shady,
but not half as cool as *ma soeur*.

Two Faces of the Sásq'ets
For some, folkloric kitsch,
for others, *Gigantopithecus
blacki*, a Bering land bridge
migrant who's still with us.
for Michael Medved

In the Ring
Skeffington liked getting things done—not to mull over details, but to make deals. He was a true pol.
after Edwin O'Connor

Hamsa Hand
It takes the indifference
of a callous man
to refuse the assistance
of this talisman.

The Clocks Unwind Like Mild Horses Tracing Circles Inside a Corral

"Even the mare horse is a kind of man,"
wrote William Faulkner, as if every equine
was part of a Centaur god's master plan.
Try the opposite: a gorgeous neckline,
delicate ankles, the fluttering eyelashes—
even the biggest stud in the corral
can play a lady. Vanity improves morale
for us all: man, woman, horse that flashes
her mane in the light of August ... Skeigh,
fittingly—it's when broken we are meek.

Beauty & Money
Good looks matter to both girls and boys,
and money for each is the perfect counterpoise.

He Chews His Own Toenails

He had terrible athlete's foot
and (whenever he ran) asthma. Boric
acid helped heal his hoof,
but made jogging phantasmagoric.

You Have Got to Be Kidding
Alchemy, astrology, baraminology, all dodgy
pseudo-sciences. But the worst is phrenology.

Desperation After the Dumping

After she broke it off, he called her all
day long, leaving messages of pure falderal.

Wittgenstein's Hut
On a hillside in Norway,
there is an austere cabin
overlooking a fjord,
built above silent stones
beside a small sward.

To Ear is Human
Who else could put on a mouse chattel
that looks like a saddle?
for J. Vacanti, C. Vacanti, Bob Langer & the Mouse

Cape Fear, Delaware, January 15, 1865: Confederate Lieutenant Colonel Ezekiel Abernathy Confronts General Robert Hoke During the Second Battle of Fort Fisher

"Snatch your saddle or pick your paddle,
either way we's got to skedaddle!"

Crazy Expensive
One week as an analysand
will cost about a grand.

And That's No Bull
Art (as matador) and Tina
(his cape) tried to ennoble
a monotonous routine
with a fine paso doble.

He Who Struggles with God
Confronted by a stranger
regarded later as His minion,
your hand still clutching
after the merciless pinion.

The Archer
Candid but careless,
with an inconstant, philosophical soul—
thus aims the archer
at the bull's eye within the aureole.

Basic Training for Brains
Think of your Self as a soul,
And your soul as a kind of prism
refracting light beyond the null
and void of an arid solipsism.

The Twinkie Defense Was Just Finky
As he stood,
anxiously waiting for the court to arraign
him for good,
he considered his best defense: a bad brain.
after Paul Krassner

What Else Can You Do?
After weeks of watching him win,
the house placed a ban
on his betting, which he took on the chin.
There can only be one trepan.

Name Your Favorite Scandal
The missus came to realize
how much his folly cost her:
he may not have been very wise,
but was one helluva snollygoster.

After Five Decades of Fitting In

He was used to keeping an eye on the clock.
For fifty years he had been a rock
rolled in a trommel. Late
the hour, late the man, nothing to promulgate.

Joined in Battle

The knight greets his armor—the visor, the annulate arms and legs—as an opponent who must be met.

Flipping My Brand New Nickel
than the reverse, Monticello. The obverse
has a portrait of Jefferson, gobs worse

Suffragette Forest
As humankind wrecks one
corner of the woods
after another for more goods,
animals need a voice
in setting wilderness policy.
Sharing the choice
with (at least) the ursine polity
shouldn't be verboten,
so let every last bear vote in
in the general election.

Novus Homo

With an eye out for highly public trials, Cicero
could prosecute or defend the political picaro.
for Alain Gowing

Undivine Guidance
At times my affairs are as if arranged by malign
spirits, especially when by my own design.

Better than the Squirting Flower
For comic effect, Chuckles had a curly wig
that spun above his head like a whirligig.

The Visiting Lecturer
The audience had nothing on professors in mocking
the ambitious young bluestocking.

Crying Fowl on the Capitoline Hill
They tried to sneak by, disregarding the goose. How that turned out landed them in the hoosegow.

The Holdout

He begged her for years,
his determination indubitable,
and when she turned forty
he was suddenly suitable.

Aedes Varipalpus
Assuming it was a blood orange, could a mosquito poke through its rind and the rubbery albedo?

Mexican Sonata
The milky, cinnamon flavor of horchata
lingers like a note sustained in fermata.

As the Finance Guy Always Explains
Never mind the price. You can afford a low payment, as detailed in the bordereau.

The First Law of Women's Fashion
Le plus cher the habiliments,
the fewer the filaments.
But the greater the compliments.

The Bennet Sisters

We don't mean to demean
your social status,
but if you want to date us,
you need a demesne.
after Jane Austen

Postscript to *Credences of Summer*
Belief demands a real leaf — *der gott in all*
en dingen — as September turns serotinal.
after Wallace Stevens

The Present Moment
Forever severing and pari passu
Gathering everything old and new.

Women Rule
Flowers, dinner, a glass of wine—our key
to unlocking the secrets of the gynarchy.

In Hock to the Chicoms
To obtain our quittance
will require no mere pittance.

A Bitter Farewell for a Cow
Dead after falling down
at the end of a dazed meander
that began by nibbling
blossoms of *Nerium oleander.*

Medieval Job Description
Sing how much ye doth revere her boob, adore her *derrière*, and love her leg. Wanted: troubadour.

Early One Saturday Morning
Under a stiff black bowler
and behind a vermillion cravat
a perfectly elegant stroller
stepped to the curb like a cat.
Gripping the big gray knob
of a gently planted ebony cane,
our deft little natty nabob
vaulted over an ocean of rain.

On a Beach Near Boston
We stood shoulder deep,
playing with the pull
of the tide tumbling over
the sands of the shoal.

Blockbusters Today
All those bigger explosions
and the higher high tech
take more and more money
to make even more dreck.
for Brian Bell

Benedicta
The esse
of our esse
is to bless
this esse.

Another Foil for Thine Incomparable Oil
For there on the headrest
was what looked like panties some lass wore
playing rugby in the mud,
so the porter brought a new antimacassar.
after Lord Byron

Don't Pay the Bearer on Demand
The counterfeiter
said, about a fence who'd begun to skitter,
"Back him a D
note, but make sure it's a facsimile."

George's Gentle Premonition on the 5th of July
The morning sun was filtered by trees
and clouds as he sat at a picnic table eating pecan
pie. He felt the stir of a soft breeze
on his cheek, then the first drops of a serein.
"Could be rain," he said, with no hope
it wouldn't. More pie, but then sunshine. "Nope."
i.m. George Rolfe

Trading in the Tignasse
We try hard for just the right
look, and hair means youth.
Youth can be stupid. Truth
be told though, *sans* wig, your
scalp now shines with a light
a postiche cannot transfigure.

Sundowners

Fireflies, like rabbits, barn owls, and ocelots,
are crepuscular
animals who come out at twilight, but are lots
less muscular.

Mercury Was Not a Cure for Me
When I once had a terrible cold,
an intern alchemist prescribed a broth
of roots, mushrooms and azoth.
A better metal might have been gold.

For a Few Hours, Anyway
Life seeming rather drab of late,
La Reine Margot decided to abdicate.
after Isabelle Adjani

Mashed Couch Potato in the Gravy
For the worst kind of trachle
Even consciousness becomes a shackle.

Remember the Cuckoo Clock Speech?
To Joseph Cotton's Holly
Martins, Baroness Alida Maria Laura
Altenburger von Marckenstein-Frauenberg
played Anna Smith (her
billing was simply "Valli").
Orson Welles was Harry Lime. The burg
was Vienna. Director Reed went looking for a
unique score, thus Anton Karas' zither.
after Graham Greene

Davy Jones' Locker

In the hadal
zone, does the Sea Cucumber
or the Bristle Worm
feel many tidal
forces? Do they squirm?
Or simply slumber?

Angling for Any Little Satisfaction
When his daughter finished
the day with a real lunker
he wished
he could dunk her.

Whether You Call It a Glutton, a Carcajou, or a Skunk Bear, this Beast is Fierce in Any Language

Gulo gulo makes you sick — catch
a whiff of that anal stink
and you may claw your own face
off. Fast enough to chase
a lynx, so tenacious it won't blink
from a bear. It has thick,
oily fur to keep warm and wick
away water. Stocky. About
a foot tall at the shoulder, snout
to tail, three: the quickhatch.
for Joseph O'Brien

Son of Typhon
Six fiery eyes and a scary address
had this iconic cur.
Brother to the Hydra. Try to guess
his moniker …

Light Shineth in Darkness
Whenever we played Scrabble,
we used an old Crown Royal
bag of purple felt to grabble
in dark chaos for each new tile.
i.m. Paul Gamble

Fashionable Exclamation
When the models walked
out on the runway, dressed
so tastefully in Vera Wang,
the audience wore a shocked
demeanor, best expressed
with a boldfaced interabang.
for Kristine Jawili

L'Embarquement pour Cythère (Louvre)
The ingredients for a daydream of leisure
fill this *fête galante* painted by Watteau: sea, an
island, everything lush, and a favonian
column of pink cupids borne aloft by pleasure.
after Jean-Antoine Watteau

Glossary

A

abdicate *to renounce a throne, dignity, or function*

abecedarian *a beginner in any field of learning*

abiogenesis *the origin of life from nonliving matter*

accrete *to grow; accumulate*

achromic *colorless; without coloring matter*

ad hominem *attacking an opponent's character*

ad infinitum *to infinity; endlessly; without limit*

adret *a side of a mountain receiving direct sunlight*

aggrandize *to make appear greater in power or wealth*

aglet *tag or sheath at the end of a shoelace*

agrarian *a person who favors the equal division of landed property and the advancement of agricultural groups*

ailurophilia *a liking for cats*

albacore *any of various tunalike fishes*

albedo *the white, inner rind of a citrus fruit.*

alphitomancy *the use of barley meal for divination*

ambivert *personality between introvert and extrovert*

ambulant *moving from place to place*

ambulate *to walk or move about from place to place*

Ameslan *ASL, or American Sign Language*

anagnorisis *the critical moment of recognition, discovery*

analysand *a person undergoing psychoanalysis.*

annulate *formed of ringlike segments or bands*

anon *in a short time; soon*

antebellum *before a war, esp. the American Civil War*

antediluvial *before the flood, in Noah's time*

antimacassar *ornamental cover on a headrest*
antitype *something foreshadowed by a type or symbol*
aphesis *consisting of the loss of a short unaccented vowel (as in* lone *for* alone)
apocryphal *of doubtful authenticity*
appellation *name, title, or designation*
arboreal *of or relating to trees*
arraign *to call before a court to answer to an indictment*
asyndeton *the omission of conjunctions*
aubade *a song or poem greeting the dawn*
august *marked by majestic dignity or grandeur*
aureole *the luminous area surrounding the sun or other bright light when seen through thin cloud or mist*
azoth *mercury regarded by alchemists as the first principle of metals; the universal remedy of Paracelsus*

B

banal *lacking freshness, originality, or novelty*
bedash *to splash with color*
beforetime *formerly*
bel-esprit *a person of great wit or intellect*
bemused *marked by confusion or bewilderment*
bestiary *a collection of descriptions or representations of real or imaginary animals*
blatherskite *a person given to voluble, empty talk*
bletting *fruit stored until the desired ripening is attained*
blighter *a contemptible, worthless person; scoundrel*
bluestocking *a woman with scholarly interests*
boffin *a scientist or technical expert*

boîte *a nightclub; cabaret*

bon mot *a clever remark*

boondoggle *an impractical project involving graft*

borborygmus *intestinal rumbling caused by gas*

bordereau *a detailed note or memorandum of account*

bovarism *exaggerated or glamorized estimate of oneself*

braggart *a loud, arrogant boaster*

brickle *easily broken; brittle*

brusque *blunt in manner; ungracious harshness*

bugbear *a continuing source of irritation*

C

camelopard *giraffe*

capriccio *a caper; prank*

catharsis *a purification or purgation of emotions that brings about spiritual renewal or release from tension*

caveat *a warning or caution; admonition*

cede *to yield or formally surrender to another*

chattel *a moveable article of personal property*

chiaroscuro *distribution of light and shade in a picture*

chirk *to make a shrill, chirping noise*

chutzpa *unmitigated effrontery or impudence; gall*

clairaudience *the power to hear sounds said to exist beyond the reach of ordinary experience or capacity*

claptrap *any artifice or expedient for winning applause*

cloister *any quiet, secluded place*

clowder *a group of cats*

cockalorum *a self-important little man*

cognizant *aware (usually followed by* of*)*

colloquy *a conversational exchange; dialogue*
columbine *of a dove; dovelike*
commissure *a line or point where two things are joined*
comport *to behave in a manner proper and expected*
con amore *with love, tender enthusiasm, or zest*
consanguinity *a close relation; kinship*
contiguous *touching; in contact*
contrails *streaks of condensed water vapor created in the air by an airplane or rocket at high altitudes*
coterie *a group of people who associate closely*
counterpoise *equal and opposing power; in equilibrium*
coxcomb *a conceited, foolish dandy; pretentious fop*
crapulous *characterized by gross excess in drinking*
crepuscular *of, relating to, or resembling twilight*
cuittle *to wheedle, cajole, or coax*
cummerbund *wide sash worn at the waist with a tuxedo*
cusp *a point or pointed end*
cygnet *a young swan*

D

decant *to pour a liquid from one container to another*
degust *to taste or savor carefully or appreciatively*
deipnosophist *an adept conversationalist at table*
deke *to deceive; fake an opponent out of position*
demesne *legal possession of land as one's own*
desiderium *an ardent desire or longing*
diathesis *predisposition for abnormal or diseased state*
diction *choice of words for clearness or effectiveness*
dilatory *tending to delay or procrastinate*

dilly *something or someone regarded as unusual*
disambiguate *to establish a single semantic or grammatical interpretation*
dissilient *springing apart; bursting open*
dither *to act nervously or indecisively*
divynailes *divinations*
doggerel *comic or burlesque verse, and usually loose or irregular in measure*
dreck *excrement; dung; trash; junk*
dudeen *a short clay tobacco pipe*
dyad *a group of two; couple; pair*

E
echt *real; authentic; genuine*
effloresce *to burst into bloom; blossom*
emanate *to come out from a source*
emulsify *to disperse in an emulsion*
en bloc *as a whole*
epitome *a typical or ideal example*
equanimity *evenness of mind especially under stress*
espousal *betrothal; wedding; marriage*
esse *in scholastic philosophy, actual being*
estivate *to pass the summer in a state of torpor*
euthenics *a science concerned with bettering the condition of human beings through the improvement of their environment*
evanesce *to disappear gradually; vanish; fade away*
exalted *raised or elevated, as in rank or character*

F

facsimile *an exact copy of a book, painting, or manuscript*

falderal *nonsense; foolish talk or ideas*

fallacy *a deceptive, misleading, or false notion, belief*

famulus *a servant of a scholar or magician*

favonian *of or relating to the west wind; mild or favorable*

fermata *the sustaining of a note, chord, or rest for a duration longer than the indicated time value*

fervent *having great warmth or intensity of spirit*

feuilleton *a part of a European newspaper devoted to light literature, fiction, criticism, etc.*

fiddlesticks *interjection used to express impatience*

filaments *a very fine thread or threadlike structure; fiber*

finagle *to trick, swindle, or cheat someone*

flak *antiaircraft fire; criticism; hostile reaction; abuse*

flapdragon *an old game in which the players snatch raisins, plums, etc., out of burning brandy, and eat them*

flit *to move lightly and swiftly; fly, dart, or skim along*

foofaraw *excessive amount of decoration; ornamentation*

foray *a quick, sudden attack*

forenamed *mentioned before in the same writing*

frenetic *frantic; frenzied*

fribble *to act in a foolish or frivolous manner*

frigorific *causing or producing cold*

frippery *finery in dress, especially when showy or gaudy*

frivol *to behave frivolously; trifle*

froideur *an attitude of haughty aloofness; cold superiority*

fusty *having a stale smell, moldy, musty*

fuchsia *a vivid, reddish purple*
fussbudget *a fussy or needlessly fault-finding person*

G
galligaskins *loose trousers in 16th and 17th centuries.*
gallinipper *a large mosquito*
gangle *to move awkwardly or ungracefully*
garnish *adorn, decorate, usually with food*
gelt *informal: money*
geomancy *divination by figures or geographic features*
gibbosity *a protuberance or swelling*
glib *readily fluent, often thoughtlessly or insincerely so*
gloaming *twilight, dusk (archaic:* **gloam***)*
gloze *to explain away; gloss over*
gnomist *a writer of aphorisms*
gnostic *possessing special knowledge of spiritual matters*
gobbet *a fragment or piece, especially of raw flesh*
gossamer *a fine cobweb seen on grass or bushes*
grabble *to feel or search with the hands; grope*
grammatology *the scientific study of systems of writing*
griffin *a fabled monster having the head and wings of an eagle and the body of a lion*
grimalkin *a cat*
guile *crafty or artful deception; duplicity*
gynarchy *government by women*

H

habiliments *clothing*

hadal *of or relating to the greatest ocean depths*

hibernaculum *protective case or cover for winter*

hippophile *one who loves horses*

hokum *a device to evoke a desired audience response*

hoodwink *to deceive or trick*

hoosegow *a jail*

hornswoggle *to swindle, cheat, hoodwink or hoax*

horripilation *bristling of hair on the skin*

hoyden *a boisterous, bold, and carefree girl*

humdinger *something of remarkable excellence or effect*

hurdy-gurdy *any of various mechanical musical instruments (such as the barrel organ)*

hyperhidrosis *generalized or local excessive sweating*

I

idem *the same as previously given or mentioned*

immiscible *incapable of being mixed*

impolitic *not politic, expedient, or judicious*

inchoation *an act of beginning; commencement*

indubitable *that which cannot be doubted*

infinitesimal *immeasurably small*

inglenook *a corner or nook near a fireplace*

instauration *an act of establishing something*

interabang *a punctuation mark (?)*

indomitable *that cannot be subdued or overcome*

irredentist *a member of a party in any country advocating the acquisition of a region in another country by reason of cultural, historical, ethnic, racial, or other ties*

J

jigger *a small glass of about one and a half ounces*
jilt *to cast off or reject someone capriciously*
joggle *to shake lightly; move to and fro*

K

kitsch *something of tawdry design, appearance, or content created to appeal to popular or undiscriminating taste*
klatsch *a gathering characterized by refreshments and informal conversation*
klaxon *a loud electric horn often used as a warning signal*
kloof *in South Africa, a deep glen or ravine*

L

laciniate *cut into narrow, irregular lobes; slashed; jagged*
laden *burdened; loaded down*
lallygag *to spend time idly; to loaf*
lam *to beat; thrash* or *a hasty flight, an escape*
lambent *dealing lightly and gracefully with a subject*
larder *a room or place where food is kept; pantry*
largesse *generous bestowal of gifts*
larrikin *a street rowdy; hoodlum*
loquacious *talkative*
layette *clothing for a newborn baby*

Lent *annual season of fasting and penitence before Easter*

lèse-majesté *a crime (such as treason) committed against a sovereign power*

leveret *a young hare*

leviathan *any huge marine animal, as the whale*

lingua franca *any language widely used as a means of communication among speakers of other languages*

lipogram *a written work composed of words avoiding the use of one or more specific alphabetic characters*

litigious *readily or excessively inclined to litigate*

loblolly *mire; mudhole*

lunker *a very large game fish, especially a bass*

M

malign *speak evil of; slander; defame*

mammon *material wealth or possessions especially as having a debasing influence*

maugre *in spite of; notwithstanding*

meander *a circuitous movement or journey*

meliorism *doctrine that the world tends to improve*

meta *showing or suggesting an explicit awareness of itself or oneself as a member of its category*

mickle *great; large; much*

minion *servile follower or subordinate*

mishpachah *a Jewish family or social unit including close and distant relatives*

misology *distrust or hatred of reason or reasoning*

modus operandi *method or procedure*

monad *any simple, single-celled organism*
moniker *a person's name, especially nickname or alias*
moosemilk *a cocktail of whiskey or rum and milk*
muster *an act of assembling*
mysophobia *an abnormal fear of contamination*

N

nabob *a very wealthy, powerful or influential person*
neologize *to make or use new words or create new meanings for existing words*
nettle *any plant of the genus* Urtica, *covered with stinging hairs*
noetic *of or relating to the mind*
nomenclature *the names comprising a set or system*
nosophobia *an abnormal fear of disease*
nostomania *intense homesickness*
novitiate *the state or period of being a beginner*

O

obeah *a form of belief involving sorcery; a fetish or charm used in practicing such sorcery*
obverse *the side of a coin that bears the principal design*
od *a hypothetical force formerly held to pervade all nature and to manifest itself in magnetism, mesmerism, etc.*
odontoid *of or resembling a tooth; toothlike*
oeillade *a glance of the eye*
omnium-gatherum *a miscellaneous collection*

omphaloskepsis *contemplation of one's naval*
onomasticon *a list or collection of proper names*
orrery *apparatus representing the positions, motions, and phases of the planets, satellites, etc., in the solar system*

P

pabulum *something that nourishes; food; nutriment*
Parnassian *pertaining to poetry*
panivorous *subsisting on bread; bread-eating*
pari passu *with equal step; at the same rate*
paso doble *a two-step dance to Latin-American rhythms*
passé-partout *(1) a master key; (2) a method of framing in which a picture and its frame are held together by strips of paper or cloth pasted over the edges*
Pavlovian *being or expressing a conditioned or predictable reaction*
pavonine *of or like a peacock*
penultimate *next to the last*
peregrine *foreign; alien; coming from abroad*
perpetuity *an annuity paid for life*
pettifogging *insignificant; petty*
phantasmagoric *having a fantastic or deceptive appearance, as in a dream or created by the imagination*
phenom *a phenomenon; especially a young prodigy*
philately *stamp collecting*
philology *the study of literary texts, the establishment of their authenticity, original form, and meaning*

philosophaster *a person with a superficial knowledge of philosophy who feigns a knowledge not actually possessed*

phrenology *a psychological theory based on the belief that certain mental faculties and character traits are indicated by the configurations of the skull*

picaro *a rogue or vagabond*

picayune *of little value or account; small; trifling*

pilcrow *a paragraph mark (¶)*

pilose *covered with hair*

pinion *outer part of a bird's wing; the flight feathers*

plantlet *a small plant*

ploce *emphatic repetition of a word with particular reference to its special significance*

pluvial *of or relating to rain, especially a lot of it*

poetaster *an inferior poet*

pokelogan *marshy or stagnant water*

pol *a politician, especially experience in making deals*

poltergeist *a ghost manifest in sounds such as knockings*

poultice *a soft cloth applied to the body to aid healing*

prate *to talk excessively and pointlessly; babble*

prelusive *introductory; having the form of a prelude*

prevaricator *a person who speaks falsely; liar*

prithee *used to express a wish or request*

pro tem *temporary; for the time being*

promulgate *to publish; proclaim publicly*

protoplast *the primordial living unit or cell*

prudence *caution regarding practical matters; discretion*

punnet *a small container for berries*

Q

quadrille *a square dance for four couples*
quickhatch *a wolverine*
quincunx *arrangement of five objects in a square, one in each corner, one in the middle*
quirk *a peculiarity of action or personality; mannerism*
quittance *discharge from a debt or obligation*

R

rancor *bitter resentment or ill will; hatred; malice*
rarefied *lofty; exalted; belonging to an exclusive group*
razz *to deride, make fun of, tease*
realpolitik *policy based on power rather than ideals*
rendezvous *a place appointed for assembling or meeting*
residuum *the residue, remainder or rest of something*
rifacimento *recasting of a literary or musical work*
rimple (n) *a wrinkle;* (v) *to wrinkle*
riposte *a quick, sharp return in speech or action*
rufescent *reddish, tinged with red, rufous*

S

salchow *a jump in which the skater leaps from the back inside edge of one skate, makes one full rotation of the body, and lands on the back outside edge of the other skate*
scabrous *indecent or scandalous; risqué, obscene*
schatzi *sweetheart, darling*
scherzo *in music, a movement or passage of light or playful character, typically the second or third movement*
schmaltz *sentimentalism; fat or grease from a chicken*

schuss *a straight downhill run at high speed*
scintillate *twinkle, spark, flash*
scofflaw *someone who flouts rules, conventions*
scrum *a usually brief and disorderly struggle or fight*
serein *fine rain after sunset from a cloudless sky*
serotinal *pertaining to or occurring in late summer*
sessile *attached at the base; not freely moving*
sickle *an implement for cutting grain, grass, etc.*
sidle *to edge along furtively*
simpatico *congenial or like-minded; likeable*
Sisyphean *relating to Sisyphus; unavailing task*
skedaddle *to run away hurriedly; flee*
skeigh *(of horses) spirited, inclined to shy;*
(of women) proud, disdainful
skosh *just a little, a bit*
slake *to allay thirst by satisfying*
snarky *having a rudely critical tone or manner*
snollygoster *a clever, unscrupulous person*
snood *a headband for the hair*
sobersided *solemn or serious in nature or appearance*
solander *a case for maps, plates, etc., made to resemble a*
book and having the front cover and fore edge hinged
solipsism *extreme preoccupation with and indulgence of*
one's feelings, desires, etc.; egoistic self-absorption
solstice *either of the two points in the ecliptic farthest*
from the equator; about June 21st and December 22nd
sooth *(n) truth, reality or fact; (adj) true or real*
sparge *to scatter or sprinkle*
spelunk *to explore caves, especially as a hobby*

spigot *a faucet for controlling the flow of liquid*
sprechgesang *a vocal style between speech and singing*
spumescent *foamy; foamlike; frothy*
squib *a short and witty saying; a small explosive used replicate a bullet hitting a surface*
star-crossed *thwarted by the stars; ill-fated*
stickle *to argue or haggle insistently*
strident *having a harsh sound or an irritating character*
stymie *hinder, thwart, block*
subfuscous *slightly dark, dusky, or somber*
subjoin *to add at the end, as of a list; append*
susurrant *softly murmuring; whispering*
sward *an expanse of short grass*

T
talisman *anything whose presence exercises a remarkable or powerful influence on human feelings or actions*
tarantism *an uncontrollable desire to dance*
tarradiddle *a small lie, fib; pretentious nonsense*
terminus *the end or extreme of anything*
thalassic *of or relating to seas and oceans*
thingamajig *a gadget or other thing for which the speaker does not know or has forgotten the name*
tiffin *lunch*
toothsome *pleasing or desirable; sexually alluring*
trachle *an exhausted or bedraggled person*
transfigure *to change in outward appearance*
trepan *a person who cheats or swindles others*

triumvirate *an association of three in office or authority*
troubadour *wandering singer circa 11th to 13th centuries*
truckle *to yield obsequiously*
twain *archaic term for the number two*

U
ubac *a mountain slope that receives little sunshine*
ugsome *horrid; loathsome*
umbriferous *casting or making shade*

V
vastitude *a vast expanse or space*
venerable *commanding respect because of age or dignity*
verbigeration *the constant or obsessive repetition of meaningless words or phrases*
verboten *forbidden, as by law; prohibited*
vernacularize *to render into or express in a vernacular*
vespertide *the period of vespers, evening*
viceroy *(1) a person appointed to rule a country or province as the deputy of the sovereign (2) a brightly marked American butterfly,* Limenitis archippus, *closely mimicking the monarch butterfly in coloration*
vigilant *ever awake and alert; sleeplessly watchful*
vilify *to speak ill of; defame; slander*
vinous *of, relating to, or made with wine*
viridescent *slightly green; greenish*
vittate *striped longitudinally*
votive *offered, given, etc. in accordance with a vow*

W

wamble *to move unsteadily*

wanderlust *a strong, innate desire to travel or roam*

wanion *curse; vengeance*

wayfarer *a traveler, especially on foot*

welkin *the sky; the vault of heaven (mostly lit.)*

weltanschauung *a comprehensive conception or image of the universe and of humanity's relation to it*

whippersnapper *a diminutive or presumptuous person*

whirligig *something that whirls or revolves*

wight *any living being; a supernatural being*

wildling *a wild plant, flower, or animal*

williwaw *violent storm blowing near the polar latitudes*

withershins *in a direction contrary to the natural one*

wroth *angry, wrathful; stormy, violent*

X

xanthic adj. *of, relating to, or tending toward a yellow color*

xylography *the art of engraving on wood*

xyst *a long and open portico*

Y

yarborough *a hand in bridge containing no ace or a card higher than a nine*

yawp *to make a raucous noise*

yclept *to name (past participle of* clepe)

yo-ho *used as a call or shout to attract attention*

Z

zazen *meditation in prescribed, cross-legged posture*

zither *musical instrument with sound box and strings*

zoanthropy *mental disorder in which one believes oneself to be an animal*

zedonk *offspring of a zebra and a donkey*

zephyr *a mild wind; (in lit., caps) the West Wind*

Author photo by Nathan Vass

Brian Jobe studied Classics at the University of Washington and the University of California at Santa Barbara. He is the author of the novel *Bird's Nest in Your Hair* and his writing has been featured in the *National Review, Letter X,* the *San Diego Reader,* the *Local Writer,* and *Dappled Things.* His essay on the novelist Walker Percy and Martin Heidegger was recently featured in *The Moviegoer at Fifty: New Takes on an Iconic American Novel,* available from LSU Press.

@ brianjobe at protonmail dot com

Typos, solecisms, and perhaps infelicities shall be rewarded with a mention in future printings, or even cold, hard cash.

www.ingramcontent.com/pod-product-compliance
Lightning Source LLC
Chambersburg PA
CBHW062040080426
42734CB00012B/2515